Feather Faith

T0158865

Feather Faith

A Cockatiel's Misadventure

BONNIE S. PAPADATOS

iUniverse, Inc.
Bloomington

Feather Faith
A Cockatiel's Misadventure

Photographs courtesy of the author
Cover feather photograph courtesy of the author,
professionally done by Tony Awad

and

Words and music by Libby Roderick c Libby Roderick Music 1988. Used by permission. All rights reserved. From the recording How Could Anyone, Turtle Island Records, Anchorage Alaska, www. libbyroderick.com libbyroderick@gmail.com., 907/278-6817

iUniverse books may be ordered through booksellers or by contacting:

iUniverse
1663 Liberty Drive
Bloomington, IN 47403
www.iuniverse.com
1-800-Authors (1-800-288-4677)

ISBN: 978-1-4620-4952-3 (sc)
ISBN: 978-1-4620-4954-7 (hc)
ISBN: 978-1-4620-4953-0 (ebk)

Printed in the United States of America

iUniverse rev. date: 11/28/2012

In Loving Memory of My Family

How Could Anyone

How could anyone ever tell you,
　　you were anything less than beautiful?
How could anyone ever tell you,
　　you were less than whole?
How could anyone fail to notice,
　　that your loving is a miracle?
How deeply you're connected to my soul.

—Words and music by Libby Roderick
c Libby Roderick Music 1988

CONTENTS

Cockatiels...1

Pet Shop..4

New Home Adjustments 10

Honey's Personality 12

Achilles' Name 15

Mealtimes..17

Honey Talk 20

Christmas Tree-topper...................................22

Loss and Heartbreak.....................................24

No Word..28

End of Lost 30

Feather Faith 37

Roommate? 39

Gastronomical Delights..................................47

Cousins 52

Acknowledgements

Most creative works cannot be accomplished alone. With this being said, my thanks go to Evangelos (Angelo) and Achilles; husband and son, respectively, for their loyal support and endless patience while I was often lax in doing other responsibilities during the formation of this book. I was lucky and I appreciated having Angelo as my own Greek chef as he lovingly took over the kitchen duty. Most struggling authors are not fortunate enough to have Greek gourmet cuisine waiting for them after many hours of writing and rewriting. And, Achilles, I could not have completed this book if you had not, unselfishly, given up your spare time—even after long hours at work. Your extensive computer technological knowledge and skills were absolutely instrumental in meeting my scheduled timetable.

As Honey and Lily are depicted in this story, my friend, Kitty, was my staunch Lily. She had faith in me, encouraged me, and gave freely of her time. As a veteran school teacher, Kitty's knowledge and use of proper grammar skills were invaluable assets. Even though we had been close personal friends for more than fifty years, it was still illuminating to discover some unexpressed emotions and feelings. And, at the same time, we had great fun debating whether the comma goes here or there, etc.

My sincerest thanks go to Lauren Bruce, Manager, Turtle Island Records, for her efforts in securing copyright permission to reprint Ms. Libby Roderick's lovely lyrics to *How Could Anyone.*

Last, but not least, my thanks go to Tony Awad, the vastly experienced photographer of Photo Scope Studios, Arlington, Virginia. His feather photo on the jacket cover delicately enhanced *Feather Faith.* And thanks, Tony, for understanding my urgency in meeting a deadline.

Preface

I never really gave much thought to writing. Certainly, I never thought about writing a book. However, while working toward retiring from a second full-time career, I told many stories about our pets to my friends and coworkers. As they listened to these tales, they were so entertained that they encouraged me to write about them. Upon retirement and after one pet's incredible experience, I decided to take their advice. Although it was a daunting endeavor, I did it because *Feather Faith* was a story that needed to be told.

This literary creation was like plummeting into a third career. Phew, someday, I'm really going to retire!

Introduction

Until my early teens, I grew up on farms in Michigan with my three siblings. We loved living on the farms because we had so many pets. We had a horse, cows, pigs, chickens, dogs and cats. Our parents taught us how to share the chores. We learned how to gather straw to make the barn stalls comfy for the horse and cows. We fetched hay to feed them. We fed the one rooster and twenty-plus hens, gathered eggs, and fed slop to the pigs. We had two coal-black, shepherd-mix collies (brother and sister to each other) and two blue-tick hounds (also brother and sister to each other), and four cats (I do not remember their breeds because my sister brought home any stray cat that would follow her).

I remember we rolled and played happily with our dogs and cats. However, I also remember a couple of incidents when some of our other pets were not so much fun.

One day when my sister fed the chickens, our feisty rooster (Hank) did not take kindly to her presence near his hens. To scare her away, he flew up and pecked her face, very close to one eye! Fortunately, her eye was saved. This, of course, took my sister off the chicken-duty roster for a long time.

Another incident, which is very, very vivid in my mind, happened when my job was to fetch a pail of fresh milk from the barn and take it to the house—which was about twenty yards away. To get to the house, I needed to go through the pasture—where Rufus grazed. Rufus was our bull calf, which we named because he was rough and had a mean temperament. (At that time, I was young with long, fiery-red hair.) Rufus did not like the color red. He espied me! Our eyes met and he immediately began chasing me. I dropped the pail of fresh milk, which splashed all over me, and ran faster than you could say the rhyme, "Jack be nimble, Jack be quick; Jack jump over the candlestick." Rufus caught up with me, butted me in the rear with his head, and helped me over the top of the fence. I plopped, face first, into a mud hole! My older brother stood nearby and laughed and laughed. He said I looked like Neapolitan ice cream—my red hair representing the strawberry ice cream, the milk representing the vanilla ice cream, and the mud representing the chocolate ice cream. I was not so amused. I learned thereafter to always have my head covered with a large bandana—not red!

The past brings to mind one particular sad memory our family endured. Our dogs followed us around the farm as we did our chores. One day, after we gathered our pails and pitchforks, we called each of the four dogs by name to come join us. Three dogs excitedly came running to us. Our beloved collie, named "Coalie," was nowhere to be found! We searched and searched for him. Months later, our family was out for a Sunday drive through the countryside. As we rode down a small dusty road, a dog barked and barked as it followed our car. When we turned our heads around, we recognized the dog as Coalie! Someone had stolen our dog! My father parked the car on the road's shoulder in front of a farm, and got out to see if the dog was really our Coalie. As he stepped around behind the car, he saw an angry man, carrying a rifle, walking down his driveway toward us. The angry man was yelling at us to move along. My father got back in the car and quickly drove away. We kids cried to leave Coalie behind, but my father saved us from a dangerous man. We, at least, knew then that Coalie had not been killed, but had been living somewhere else. Hopefully, happy.

All the crises, events, and experiences in this story are true and express the range of emotions that our family has endured and enjoyed while owning these cockatiels (so named, Honey and Lily).

Cockatiels

This book is not intended to offer any form of expertise relating to the history, breeding, purchasing, handling and care-taking, etc., of grey cockatiels. It is just a story to share the joys of having them as pets.

Cockatiels are exotic members of the parrot family. They are bred throughout the country. In-depth information pertaining to the care of cockatiels can be found in a multiple of reference sources (handbooks and manuals, as well as many web site locations). Some interesting information about them are that they:

- Can live in the wild, but also exist happily indoors as pets,
- Have an average life span of fifteen to twenty years, although some have been known to live even longer,
- Have mild temperaments and, generally, docile and charming personalities,

- Can be tamed to learn human words, short phrases and different whistle tones, and
- Can be trained to echo a variety of sounds with many different pitches.

Having never owned cockatiels, we learned many interesting, proper, and necessary care-taking facts while nurturing our pets:

- Molting is the shedding (replacing) process of old feathers, which happens several times throughout the year.
- Preening is the cleaning process of their bodies to waterproof and condition their feathers for flight, warmth, and skin-protection. You may hear an occasional screech when they have preened too close.
- Clipping their wings is necessary to avoid accidents.
- Clipping the sharp tips of their nails is easy and needs to be done once in a while with a human nail-clipper. Styptic powder should be kept nearby in case bleeding occurs.
- Trimming beaks is needed if a cockatiel has a chronic disease. Otherwise, keeping a cuttlebone

attached to the bird cage will help to keep the beak at the proper size and shape.

Our cockatiels were bred in Pennsylvania and, at six weeks old, distributed to pet stores in Virginia near our home. Fortunately, these beautiful birds were available for purchasing as pets.

Pet Shop

Our story begins on one beautiful, sunny afternoon in June of 1997. To satisfy his endless longing and pleas for a pet, we took our twelve-year-old son, Achilles, shopping to fulfill his desire. It was something we had been planning to do for a long time. In the past, Achilles had experienced some unpleasant encounters with dogs and one particular cat. He didn't want either of these for a pet. We had spent a lot of time talking about what the best choice would be for him and we were ready to go shopping.

After visiting several pet shops, Achilles was always thoroughly captivated and enthralled while browsing the bird section. He was mesmerized by their beauty, and he enjoyed listening to the conversations they seemed to be having with each other. He loved their songs and the repetitiveness of the sounds.

We visited the various pets in the store, but we always returned to the cockatiel cages. There were grey, yellow, and white cockatiels—all with bright, colorful markings on their faces. We loved the different personalities; some were very shy, and others were quite outgoing. The outgoing ones would fly and cling to the front of the cage to be closer to us. We had a good time watching the cockatiels as they played, rested, and watched us, as we watched them. They all looked so beautiful that it was difficult to choose just one.

Suddenly, we observed one of the larger, grey cockatiels fancying a smaller, grey one. At the time, we didn't know the sex difference between male and female birds, but we watched and decided that the larger bird had to be the cock (male bird). His body was slightly larger than most of the other cockatiels, and he had a broader shoulder area.

This grey male would scrunch up his wings and strut around like he thought he was a king. On the spot, we named him "Mr. King of the Cage." As well, we felt we needed to put a name to the small grey cockatiel. She seemed to want to be left alone. For the moment, we decided to call her "Miss Shy."

As we continued to watch this interaction, Mr. King of the Cage appeared to think to himself, *I like beautiful, little Miss Shy. I think I'll introduce myself and try to make her smile. I will show her my grand wings of grey, black, and white. I will show her how they can spread open wide to embrace her. Certainly, she will notice how strong and handsome I am.* He moved toward her, and he pecked her lightly with his beak to get her attention. From the angry glare in Miss Shy's eyes, it seemed she was not impressed with this neighbor. She appeared to think that he was too assertive and had a forward, aggressive attitude. She squawked loudly at this bold and brazen neighbor and quickly ran away.

Being rebuffed by Miss Shy really angered Mr. King of the Cage. He tried again to get her attention. Miss Shy moved away from him. Again, he approached her. Miss Shy turned to face him, glared at him with fury in her eyes, opened her beak, and exhaled a strong huff that clearly could not be misunderstood but to mean *Leave me alone!*

We laughed at the birds as we watched this confrontation. It being apparent that Miss Shy had tugged at my son's heart, Achilles said, "Mom, I want Miss Shy. I want to love her and protect her from Mr. King of the Cage." Decidedly, there was no hesitation but to take her home with us.

Once we purchased Miss Shy and put her in a box for the ride home, we decided she must have a different name because she did not seem to be shy with us. In the car riding home, each time we talked to her, we unconsciously called her "Honey." Thus came about a new name for this beautiful grey cockatiel with the bright yellow and white markings on her head and the beautifully applied, bright orange patch on each cheek.

When we arrived home, my son was anxious to show Honey her own room—a handsome new gilt cage, which contained two perches. One perch was positioned at the upper back part of the cage, and the other one was positioned lower at the front of the cage close enough to easily reach the three dishes for seeds, treats, and water. Honey deftly entered the cage and climbed up its opened door. She immediately appeared to feel comfortable in her new home. She paced back and forth on the upper perch a few times as if she could not believe this was her own room. Finally, she selected the upper perch on the far left side of the cage as her favorite spot to view her new family. To this day, this is Honey's favorite position in her room.

Before we left the pet store, my son wanted to buy some toys for Honey. He selected two colorful toys to hang from the top of the cage. One hanging toy consisted of two brightly painted balls, a wooden twig for perching, and a tiny shiny bell at the bottom that would ring each time Honey would climb it. She played with this toy most of the time. She quickly learned how to make the bell ring, even when she was not perched on it. She would sit on the lower perch close to her seeds' dish and would reach for the bell positioned at the very bottom of the toy. She would grab the little bell ringer with her beak and swing it back and forth to make the music. We could see by the shining gleam in her eyes that this music made her so happy. She would ring the bell with her beak for more than five minutes at a time. The bell did not ring loudly, so we enjoyed the music as much as she did.

After Honey was settled into her new room, we enjoyed the rest of the afternoon watching her become familiar with her new surroundings, while becoming acquainted with us.

About 7:30 PM that evening, Achilles covered Honey's room with a small tablecloth. He told her that her day had been long and that she needed to rest her beautiful body. He kissed her goodnight on the top of her head and promised her that there would be many days to play, and that there would be no more days for Mr. King of the Cage to bother her with his aggressive behavior.

New Home Adjustments

While heading home, Honey was very calm and content. Upon arriving at our house, she continued to display her sweet, quiet nature. She neither screeched bird talk nor fluttered and flapped her wings. We were very happy that Honey was not afraid of us.

Cockatiels generally bond quickly with one or more family members, but they often choose just one person. When Honey came to live with us, she bonded with each of us within one week. We were very pleased that she embraced all three of us.

We thought we were being excellent caretakers. We cleaned her cage and provided fresh food and water every day. However, during the first three days, Honey did not move very much from her favorite position on the upper perch. When the cage was uncovered, we did not see her eat or drink. We were worried because we thought she would starve. When we consulted our book on caring for cockatiels, we discovered that many very young cockatiels have not learned how to feed themselves and are used to being spoon-fed. Obviously, this was true of Honey. However, we learned that she, being very smart, decided that she must learn to fetch her own food. On the fourth day, we actually observed her eat seeds from the dish.

This was one of many events when we discovered just how smart birds can be. In the days ahead, we were soon to learn more from this beautiful bird.

Honey's Personality

For the first few months, our family really enjoyed watching Honey as she developed her own unique habits and personality traits. Gradually, we settled into a comfortable routine.

I worked full-time, Achilles went to school, and Angelo worked in his shop on special projects. Honey soon became adjusted to our schedules and was always excited to see us when we returned home. With her eyes aglow, she chirped excitedly and paced back and forth on a perch. We loved surrounding her with attention, which she never seemed to get enough.

Honey had a way of establishing our routines. Always, before he went to school, Achilles took her out of her cage and they talked/chirped for a few minutes. As Achilles ate his breakfast, Honey kept him company by sitting on his shoulder and pecking at his hair, as if she were combing it. He then said goodbye and let her know that they would play again when he came home.

A routine Honey and I enjoyed together centers around a grey-toned, Berber, winter jacket that was soft and cuddly. On cool days, I wore the jacket to work. Every time I put on the jacket, Honey chirped and screeched excitedly. She loved the touch of the fabric as much as I did. Before I left for work, I went to the cage and placed the jacket sleeve close enough for her to feel. Her eyes gleamed with excitement as she nipped at it, and she continued her happy screeching. When I returned home, she greeted me with the same excitement. So, before I hung the jacket in the closet, we played out the morning routine. Then, I was allowed to put it away in the closet. I told her that one day I would give her the jacket, and she could use it to make herself a nice, soft nest.

Some routines were never established. One day, Angelo let Honey out of the cage to fly around so she could exercise her wings. That particular afternoon, he sat at the dining room table working on one of his personal projects. Honey was having a joyful time flying around the rooms: out of the living room—down the hallway—back to the living room—out to the kitchen. Swish, swish, swish! Then, finally, she ended up in the dining room to light on Angelo's shoulder. He acknowledged her presence with our family bird talk, "Chee, Chee!" Honey paced back and forth across his shoulders and climbed up and perched on one of his ears. While there, curious as she was, she espied something interesting in Angelo's ear. Positioned from the top of his ear, she lowered her head and grabbed onto what had interested her. Angelo painfully uttered, "Ou . . . . ch!" To his dismay, the interesting something turned out to be one of his ear hairs. As a result, Honey learned the quick way to end her free play time.

Achilles' Name

"Achilles, Achilles, Achilleeeees!" Honey would beckon to Achilles. When he did not hear, pay attention, or get her immediately, she would call out to him again with a sharper, more impatient tone. It was funny to hear my words and distinctive tones coming from this tiny bird. She learned this increase in inflection from my repetitive requests for Achilles when he would not respond promptly.

I would open the cage door for Honey to allow her to go to Achilles. As I approached the cage, she would begin pacing rapidly back and forth. With her beak open wide, she would make short, huffing sounds of impatience, much like humans do when they release impatient sighs. When the cage door finally opened, Honey, in a big hurry, left the cage and flew in circles around the living room a couple of times to get her sense of direction. She then flew down the hallway to the bedrooms, turned left at the end of the hall, and turned right at the doorway into Achilles' room. Honey had learned the layout of the house quickly, and this was the route that she knew would take her to where she wanted to go.

With Achilles in view, she flew to him and perched on his head or shoulder. Then they would begin their fun talking (chirping) with each other. Honey's eyes would sparkle brightly, a smile almost visible on her face. As they talked and played together, she would walk across his shoulders, climb to his chest to be held, and lower her head—coaxing him to rub her head feathers. She would chirp in one tone while Achilles would try to imitate the sound. They often would play together like this for more than fifteen minutes at a time.

Mealtimes

When we dined, Honey enjoyed having her meals at the same time, either in her cage or at the table!

One evening, Achilles and I planned to have our dinner in the living room as we watched a particular TV special. We opened Honey's cage to give her an opportunity to spend some time outside the cage. At times, she liked to move outside the cage freely. She would climb up and down the sides, or perch atop the cage enjoying her freedom. As we settled down to eat, I noticed her looking from Achilles to me, eyeing our dinner plates. Her wing movements indicated that she was about to join one of us. I said, "No, Honey, this is our dinner time. Go back to your cage and eat your own food." She responded, "Chirp, chirp," and continued to eye us, looking from one person to the other. It appeared that she was trying to decide, *Whose plate do I prefer?* Suddenly, Honey flew straight to me, landed on my knee, climbed slowly up from my leg to my arm, moved down to my hand, and positioned herself next to the rim of my dinner plate. I shooed her away. "Chirp, chirp," Honey shrieked again as she flew back to her cage. She returned to try again to have dinner with me. I shooed her away for the second time. Again, she shrieked as she returned to her cage. This time she waited, watched me carefully, decided not to give up, and flew back a third time. When Honey really wants something, she is very persistent. In the end, I gave in to her persistence and separated food, just for her, on a portion of the plate. Honey ate the food, never moved away from her selected spot at my plate. Her eyes sparkled with delight. She seemed to enjoy this change in her dinner menu.

A friend once asked how we knew which foods Honey would like. By observing Honey, I gathered she preferred foods that resembled seeds. Her favorites seemed to be corn, canned peas, and tiny parts of broccoli and cauliflower florets. She was never displeased with any kind of fresh bread. She also particularly liked French-fried potatoes, which we opened so she could devour the inside, softer content. Soon, we started setting aside food favorites that Honey relished. She began to join us at the table, sitting on her table mat, and eating at her very own plate!

Honey also wanted to drink from our glasses or cups when we had iced tea, water, wine, or Greek coffee. What do you think happened? Yep, she became quite a connoisseur of Greek wines. Now, she needed her very own demitasse cup!

It was not always food that drew Honey's attention. Sometimes, she would fly over and perch on someone's shoulder. "Ouch," the victim would cry out. Honey's keen eyesight had espied what appeared to be a seed to her but was really someone's skin tag! Ouch, Ouch!

Honey Talk

When I worked full-time, each morning before I left, I approached the cage and had a small talk with Honey. I told her that I loved her, but I needed to go to work and would be back soon. As if she understood, she responded with light chirping. She would continue chirping and whistling as I walked to my car. From outside, I responded to her shrill chirps. Honey continued chirping until I pulled out of the driveway. She seemed to be saying, *Please take me with you*—or—*Please don't go*. It was very sad to leave her alone, and I wondered how she would entertain herself.

From her cage near the window, she saw my car pulling away from the house. She also saw my car as I came home and rounded the corner at the end of the street. She recognized it, and she watched as I came up the street and pulled into the driveway. After parking and getting out of the car, I heard Honey as she began to whistle and chirp. We whistled back and forth until I entered the house. Then Honey knew I was home for the day. I would think to myself, *There cannot be a more wonderful way to unwind from all the work day's frustrations than hearing the lyrical greeting from Honey's happy whistling and chirping!*

Christmas Tree-topper

Christmas had always been a special time for us, and we were happily engaging in all the many holiday traditions. We were busy inside and outside: decorating the house, buying and wrapping gifts, baking all our favorite holiday treats, and enjoying the sensuous aroma of special edible treats.

With Honey as part of our family, Christmas became even more special and entertaining. It soon became apparent that it was also a special time for her. Her eyes sparkled brightly when she looked at the small, table-sized tree that we had decorated with miniature flashing lights, glittery tinsel, and shiny, ball ornaments. One evening when we opened Honey's cage, she flew immediately to this brightly decorated tree and perched on the high tip of the tree. Suddenly, she became our official tree-topper! Her eyes smiled radiantly, embellishing the bright lights stranded around the tree. On the entertainment center, next to her cage, there was a small, ceramic, red church with a black roof and a white-tiered steeple. Lights were glowing from the tiny windows. She flew to this church and perched on top of the roof. Looking back, I think she sensed an inner faith spreading from inside this beautiful structure.

Honey's actions were breathtaking to watch during this most celebrated and meaningful season.

Loss and Heartbreak

It was a beautiful day on July 1, 2007. I was getting ready to clean house in preparation for my son's birthday on July 4th. It was about 10:00 in the morning. As I gathered cleaning materials to clean our two bathrooms, I found myself gasping for air, my head feeling very light, and suddenly my heart began beating rapidly. As I thought I had not done anything to cause this sensation, I sat down for a short rest. When I felt better, I tried to continue with the chores. Not two minutes later, the same spell occurred and I found I needed to rest again to regain my normal heartbeat rate. I realized that something was seriously wrong. As long as I was in a resting position, I was comfortable and felt no need to place an emergency call for help. I was not happy to delay the household chores, but I did not want my condition to worsen. I decided to forego the cleaning and rest until my son came home from work.

Achilles arrived home shortly after six o'clock in the evening. He asked how I was doing because he saw me resting in the chair, and he wondered why I was not beginning to fix dinner—as was my usual routine at this time. When I told him of my day, he insisted on taking me to the hospital and having a doctor exam me to make sure everything was fine. After about two hours of observation in the emergency room, doctors felt an overnight stay was necessary to determine what was causing the lightheadedness and the rapid heartbeat spurts. Intensive tests were performed the next day, and the overnight stay became a stay that lasted several days. Doctors discovered blood clots in both lungs. Treatment required constant medical attention and absolute complete bed rest. While I was dismayed not to be going home and possibly missing my son's birthday, I was sure that following doctors' orders would ensure a quicker recovery and an earlier release.

Meanwhile, at home on the Fourth of July holiday, my son let Honey out of the cage to get her daily exercise. My husband went outdoors for a short period to enjoy the pleasant summer evening.

As it got darker and darker, many firecrackers were heard exploding around the neighborhood. Honey flew from one room to another, heard the noises from the firecrackers, and became spooked and afraid. She screeched loudly as she flew frantically all over the house. Meanwhile, my husband came back into the house. Before he closed the door, another firecracker exploded. Honey, circling nearby, became afraid and disoriented. As Angelo came in, Honey flew out! Out into the dark, frightening night! Out into the loud, scary noises of firecrackers! Also lurking were menacing dangers from wild, night animals and stalking birds of prey. Additionally threatening to Honey was the extremely hot summer temperature.

The night to celebrate this Fourth of July, and Achilles' birthday, suddenly became a night of loss and heartbreak. Immediately, Angelo and Achilles began searching for Honey. They did not see in the dark night where she had flown. Calling out for Honey, they searched and searched throughout the neighborhood.

After several hours, Angelo and Achilles returned home with heavy, heavy hearts because they were unable to bring Honey with them. They had not phoned me for the evening because they did not want to bring sad news to me, but they knew that I would be upset to find out they had kept this news from me. Upon hearing of Honey's sudden departure into the unknown night and extreme heat, my heart was broken, and I was filled with fear of what was to become of her. Hauntingly, my childhood memory of losing the family shepherd-mix collie dog, Coalie, loomed chillingly before my eyes. I was also frustrated not to be home to console my family and to help in their search for Honey. Their holiday and birthday celebration had been ruined. They were devastated and worried about how Honey would survive in the unfamiliar environment. With it being Achilles' birthday, it was the worst day in his life to have lost our beloved bird!

Finally, after all their efforts of searching and calling for Honey were unsuccessful, Achilles phoned the Virginia animal shelter to report that she was lost. As nighttime deepened, we prayed for Honey's safe return. Sadly, all that remained at home of Honey's presence, lying starkly in the middle of the living room floor, was one of her important flight tail feathers that had become forcefully detached during her frantic flight!

No Word

Still missing! Achilles continued for days to search for Honey in the neighborhood. As each day passed and he returned home without her, his heart grew heavier and heavier. He felt that he was to blame for her loss. He thought that he should have foreseen the possibility of the fireworks creating a frightening scene.

Because Angelo and Achilles had searched extensively and because they did not hear word from the animal shelter, we were sure that Honey was gone forever. We were devastated. To console Achilles and to fill the void in our broken hearts, I convinced him to buy another cockatiel. Thus, we adopted and welcomed a cousin of Honey's into our home, another grey cockatiel. She adjusted nicely to her surroundings and especially bonded quickly with Achilles and Angelo. She loved to play with Achilles, letting him chase her around the house while she was out of the cage exercising her wings. Afterwards, she flew to Angelo to be held. She bent her head down for him to lightly rub her head feathers, and her eyes sparkled each time he did this. Hopefully, the new addition would begin the healing process needed to adjust to Honey's loss.

Finally, on July 10, 2007, I was released from the hospital. Welcoming me home was this beautiful grey cockatiel, ten years younger than Honey and with almost identical physical markings. And, wow, did she like to sing! Because her singing brought to mind the much-loved Manfred Mann song, *Hi Lili, Hi Lo*, we named her Lily.

End of Lost

R-r-r-ring! R-r-r-ring! The ringing phone jostled our quiet, Sunday morning on July 22, 2007. Unbeknownst to us, these sounds were to announce an amazing, truly eventful day in our lives.

Achilles answered the phone and said that the phone call was for him. Without knowing the details of the phone call, I naturally assumed the call was from one of his friends. Shortly thereafter, he announced he was going out for a couple of hours. When he said "Bye" as he left the house, my assumption was that he was leaving to meet his friend.

Achilles went to his car, mapped out an address on his navigation system, and began a trip to an unfamiliar area in Maryland. He headed North on I-495 toward Baltimore and got on Maryland Route 210, which took him to his final destination of Bryans Road in Charles County, Maryland.

Achilles informed me later that the earlier phone call came from a family residing in Charles County, nearly twenty-five miles from where we live in Alexandria, Virginia. During the phone conversation, they reported that they found a cockatiel on the shore of the beach. When they checked with their local animal shelter and described the physical characteristics of the found bird, they were told that there was no record of a lost cockatiel in their immediate area. The family was then referred to a Virginia animal shelter for assistance in locating the missing bird's family. The Virginia shelter reported that they received a call on the Fourth of July holiday that a grey cockatiel escaped from a house when a door was opened. The animal shelter also stated that, as of July 22, 2007, the cockatiel was still listed as missing. The Maryland family was provided with the telephone number to contact the Virginia family. They called to let us know that they found a cockatiel and then graciously provided directions to their home in Charles County. They invited Achilles to come and see the bird. If he could make an accurate identification, then he would be free to take her home.

While Achilles drove towards Charles County, he remembered the happy times of playing, talking and whistling with Honey, as well as the lowest, depressed feelings when losing her. Also, rushing through his mind were feelings of anxiety, fear, sadness, and anticipation of what might be waiting for him when he reached what seemed to be an endless destination. His thoughts were: *Will the bird be Honey? Will she recognize me? Will the family release her if they feel my identification of her is insufficient? How will I feel if I have to return home without Honey? Can I bear losing her again?* So many emotional thoughts and questions to be answered; it was almost too overwhelming to contemplate. Lastly, he thought to himself, *Soon, I will know. Certainly, God hasn't led me this far to disappoint me at this stage of the journey.*

Upon arrival at the Charles County address, Achilles immediately recognized the very battered bird as Honey and pointed out her particular facial and body markings. He eagerly looked for signs of recognition of his face or his voice. There were none!

The family relayed to Achilles how they found this weakened and physically battered bird struggling, with every ounce of its strength and power to get close to the water's edge for a drink. Because of the bird's weakened condition, the family was able to capture the bird. Their children immediately became protective of the bird, loved it, and wanted to keep it. However, the parents felt that they must find the rightful owners of the cockatiel because they must surely be distressed over the loss of their bird—which we were indeed. Also, since the bird was so frail, they thought it would heal better in its own home environment. They tenderly cared for the bird's health the best they could, while hoping the bird's owners would soon be found.

After telling Achilles these details, the family then gingerly packaged Honey into a shoe box and lovingly turned her over to him for safe transportation back to Virginia where she could get immediate medical attention.

Achilles headed the car down the road in the direction of Virginia. Honey was settled in the shoe box and placed in the front seat with the belt securely buckled. As Achilles quickly sped away from Maryland, he heard huffing, hissing, and sobbing-like sounds coming from the box. He was sure Honey was afraid of being boxed in and fearful of what was happening. As he drove, he talked and talked to her to try to calm her. Praying and hoping for Honey's well-being, he planned his first stop to be a veterinarian hospital for an evaluation of her present condition. The doctor immediately took Honey to a laboratory room for an examination and X-rays. As in any hospital, Achilles nervously paced the waiting room area for the doctor to return with his analysis and results. He finally returned, in what seemed an interminable length of time, and stated that Honey was extremely dehydrated, very weak, and much-traumatized. (Wildlife officials report that Fourth of July and New Year's Eve revelers shooting off fireworks often startle birds and cause them to die from stress.) Her X-rays did not indicate any broken bones. He gave Achilles instructions for her care, and he sedated Honey to make her more comfortable for the rest of her journey.

Achilles arrived home in the early afternoon. As he entered the house, he called out to me in an alarming tone, and I immediately hurried to the living room to see what was wrong. He held a shoe box, with some holes in the sides. I thought perhaps he had shopped for shoes. As I approached, he lifted the top off the shoe box and lifted up an old washcloth which covered something inside. As he completely removed the washcloth, I gasped with shock to see Honey cowering inside in a corner of the shoe box. As immediate thanks were offered to God for Honey's safe return, uncontrollable tears of joy flowed down my face. Home at last! Home at last!

After being missing for such a long time, Honey was nearly unrecognizable. Although she did not have any broken bones, she suffered from an injured wing. Some of her feathers were missing, some were bent and askew, and some were just barely hanging on. If a sudden strong breeze happened, it would have been able to blow many more feathers away. She was so very thin, and her body had shrunk in size. Living for so many days in the outdoor weather elements had taken a toll on her body, and her suit color had faded greatly. The breast and other areas of Honey's body, which used to be deep charcoal grey in color, were now ashen grey. Also, her beautiful facial markings were not as bright as before. The harsh summer weather made the areas around her eyes appear wrinkled and tired-looking, much how people age from too much sun exposure. While others found Honey's physical condition repelling and hopelessly in dire straits, we still found her to be the beautiful bird we lost nineteen days previously—even more so because of how she endured so bravely such a devastatingly, mind-bogglingly adventure.

As the veterinarian stated, Honey's body was much-traumatized. The empty, distant stare displayed her depression, mixed with fear and intimidation by her current surroundings. We wanted to hold, comfort, and love Honey to reassure her that she arrived safely home, but we knew we would only frighten her more with any sudden movements. We kept our distance for Honey to bond anew with us. Our guard began as we observed Honey for any signs of deterioration and improvement.

Feather Faith

Honey was still a baby when we brought her home. When pets are adopted and welcomed into your home, they immediately become your children. You, therefore, talk to them lovingly, as you would with your small child. Thus, one will understand my evening talks with Honey.

As I prepared to cover her cage at bedtime, my nightly litany was, "Are you ready for bed? Do you have your jammies (pajamas) on? Have you said your prayers?" Honey responded with a chirp after each question. When I retired for the night, no matter what the hour, I said to her, "Jesus loves you. Mommy, Achilles, and Daddy love you. Sweet dreams, Baby." I then gave Honey my human chirp sign-off, "Chee, Chee." She always responded with one last soft chirp. It was as if she understood what I had communicated to her. Then, I knew Honey would sleep peacefully through the night and be comforted with Jesus' presence and love. I felt that this nightly ritual provided Honey with the faith that Jesus was watching over her—as we feel God's presence.

When Honey was at her lowest and saddest time of her life, the Lord felt that faith and reached down to a young family, who was enjoying the beach located near their home in Charles County, Maryland. He guided them to this lost, helpless, and battered bird.

We are so thankful and grateful for this Good Samaritan family. We are especially grateful for their good sense and compassion in seeking an animal shelter in Virginia for assistance in locating Honey's owners. With God's saving graces and blessings, along with the help of this family, a small, physically battered, weather-beaten bird was rescued and manifested itself into another one of God's miracles. God recognized Honey's "feather faith." He guided and protected her, confirming His presence and love for all mankind, animals, and other living creatures.

Roommate?

We knew that Honey realized she was home from the way that she looked at her cage, with a slight bend of her head and a slight twitch of a tail feather. As she looked at it, she huffed and glared at something—another bird sitting on her perch!

Achilles introduced the new cage occupant, Lily, to Honey. She did not welcome this new occupant in her cage, so she continued to huff and glare at Lily. Because of the traumatized condition brought on by the outdoor adventure, Honey needed to be alone to feel safe and secure. Since Lily was unknown to Honey, she must have represented another threatening bird of prey.

While in the outside world for nineteen days, Honey developed a survivalist's nature. To protect Lily from Honey's current wild-natured temperament, caused because of a harsh habitat, we put Lily in an old, parakeet bird cage that we pulled from storage.

Later, we purchased another cockatiel cage in case it became necessary for separate housing.

We placed the two bird cages side by side. Honey seemed to feel safe by being alone in her cage, though she remained quiet and subdued. She did not move from the upper corner perch and remained still and silent throughout the night. Lily watched Honey closely, seeming to know she was not well. Lily displayed neither signs of fear nor aggression toward Honey. She just watched Honey with concern and wonderment, as we also were doing.

From Honey's outward appearance, we knew she must have been unwelcomed by many other bird families and must have fought many battles to survive. So, we decided to let her recuperate in her own way. She was totally quiet the whole first and second days, she drank very little water, and she appeared not to be eating. For those two days, we closely watched Honey for changes in her behavior. She moved slowly from side to side on her perch. So as not to alarm Honey, we let her be alone to learn again that this was her safety zone.

In the past, we made a whistling sound that is commonly known as a "wolf whistle." Honey liked the sound and often echoed it repeatedly. On the second day of her return home, I decided to make the wolf whistle sound to see if Honey would recognize it and echo it as she had done in the past. Realizing Honey's trauma, it would not have surprised me if she could not do so, but she seemed to, and she acknowledged the sound with a slight twitch of her head feathers. This gave me gleeful hope that she had not lost her total memory. However, efforts to help Honey recognize Achilles' name were unsuccessful. In the meantime, Lily continued with her attempts to talk to her. Honey still would not respond to Lily's offer of friendship.

On the third day, she sat in the corner of her perch, came down occasionally to drink a little water, and ate a few seeds. Then she would return to the perch corner. We talked softly to Honey throughout the day. She did not respond, but she seemed to welcome our voices by cocking her head upward at an angle as she looked at us as if wondering what we were trying to communicate with her.

Honey continued, on the fourth day, to eat a small amount of seeds as well as to drink small amounts of water more often. She made her first attempt to speak, which was a softly uttered chirp. She was still very timid and afraid. With the sudden jerking of her head feathers, she still showed slight recognition of the wolf-whistle sound. Also, for the first time, I noticed her head feathers twitch slightly when I mentioned Achilles' name. She left the safety of the perch and came to the front of the cage. This gave us a sigh of relief because it was a sign that she wanted more attention. All this time, Lily waited patiently for Honey to join in her chatter.

About 8:00 AM on the fifth day, there was a soft chirping sound from Honey, which we interpreted was a way to let us know that she wanted the cage cover removed and the draperies opened. In the past, this was her way to welcome the new day. We knew this was another good sign in her recovery. Later that evening when we were all out of the room at the same time, Honey beckoned us for attention with much stronger chirping. We cheered excitedly as she did this, another improvement in her health! We were also pleased to see Honey eating more seeds than she had eaten in the previous days.

Many nights, Honey began periods of very faint wailing, almost as if crying. It was as if she was fearful of what the night might bring her way. Hearing her soft wailing broke our hearts, and we felt so helpless in comforting her. To let her know she was not facing fears and demons alone, we spoke softly to her until she became calm.

The sixth day was welcomed again by Honey's soft request to uncover the cage and open the curtains. This sign of progress was welcomed each new day, as we looked for more signs of recovery in her health and memory.

At last, on the seventh day, Lily and Honey began talking to each other. Lily's voice was strong and musical. Honey's voice was weak and scratchy.

On the eighth day, Lily was placed in Honey's cage for a short period of time. Finally, they actually seemed to enjoy each other's company. Lily even seemed to sense that Honey was still not completely well. They then chirped back and forth for a long time.

Occasionally, our cockatiels liked to have someone rub their head feathers. In the past when Honey wanted them rubbed, she would let us do it. Now when she wants this done, Honey moves very close to Lily and lowers her head. Lily seems to understand, and with her beak she willingly rubs Honey's head feathers. This affectionate gesture is one of many ways that Lily comforts and pleases Honey. However, when Lily wants her head feathers rubbed, she only lets Angelo or Achilles do it.

While Honey was in the wild, she learned many different, unusual songs from other bird families. Now that Lily shared Honey's cage, Honey taught Lily these songs. At first when Honey came home, she sang the same songs over and over and over and over again. Lily learned Honey's songs quickly and sang the songs with Honey over and over and over and over again. At last—communication was established between the two birds. Yes, the cacophony was deafening at times.

Several days passed with no more significant changes in Honey's behavior. It seemed that she was beginning to feel more comfortable in her home. On the eleventh night, Lily and Honey officially became roommates. There was no conflict throughout the night. Now, Honey seemed to sleep restfully with Lily's presence nearby.

Each day, Honey and Lily welcomed the mornings with light chatter. They became our duet, singing the many different dialects. Our home began to sound like a deep forest, with myriad bird species.

After two weeks of observing Honey's movements and behavior, we sensed a slow road to recovery. Lily became the critical nursemaid and strong influence in the recovery of Honey's health and spirit. She helped each day to build Honey's trust in us and helped her to welcome our love and attention.

Our hearts sing now that we have Honey home. As I've stated before, her outward physical appearance changed drastically. We know, with time and lots of good nutrition, her suit will become the shiny, dark one she wore so beautifully in the past.

Often I catch Honey looking at me with such deep sadness in her eyes. I wish I could trade places with her in order to better understand how she feels and to let her know that I share in her pain and suffering.

As I watch her in this state of despair, it is almost like she is reliving some past horrors. At those times, she looks at me as if she was thinking—*I should know you better. Who are you? What has happened to me? What all am I not remembering? Will my feelings of loss ever end????*

We continue to pray that her spirit will heal, and that her heart will sing with happiness as before.

Gastronomical Delights

Nudge, nudge. I stirred in bed and thought to myself, *What is pushing me? Wake up and you will know*. It was another glorious day, and the sun poked through the curtains and played games with me. Birds, indoors and outdoors, chirped good morning. Who could resist these cheerful nudges to greet the day?

As I shuffled in my slippers toward the kitchen, I stopped by to say good morning to the birds. Lily clung to the front of the cage door and looked as if she hoped someone would come by with a key. On the lower perch at one food dish, Honey began to eat her favorite cereal, Cheerios.

After acknowledging their good morning, I told Honey that eating Cheerios is reportedly healthy for the heart. She looked at me skeptically, with her head cocked at an angle, and continued to eat her Cheerios.

While Lily clung to the cage door, she noticed the attention I gave to Honey while she ate her breakfast.

She moved down from the door to the other food dish and started to eat the seeds. I told Lily that her food was also very good for the body, particularly in helping her to have keen eyesight and to make her dressy feathers shinier. She didn't appear to care what benefits the seeds provided, just as long as they were tasty. As she continued to eat the seeds, she kept glancing at Honey and noticed that she was really making a dent in the Cheerios—filled dish. She appeared to think, *Umm, umm, umm . . . If I don't make my move soon, there will be no Cheerios for me!*

After a few moments, Lily decided that she desperately wanted the Cheerios that Honey was eating. She pecked lightly on Honey's wing as if to ask her to make space and to share the Cheerios. Honey did not move to make room for Lily. Lily pecked at Honey's wing again and pushed her aside. Lily's appetite for Cheerios, instead of seeds, had grown tremendously. At times, Lily's temperament is somewhat jealous and aggressive. She went from the seeds dish to the Cheerios dish and began greedily eating the delicious Cheerios that Honey had been enjoying. Honey appeared to become annoyed with

Lily's rude behavior of butting in but she moved over a little more. Lily took the opportunity, nudged Honey aside even more to have the dish all to herself, and ate greedily at the Cheerios. When this happened, Honey's eyes glared with anger, and she opened her beak and huffed at Lily. Lily did not move aside to let Honey join her at the dish. As Honey watched Lily eat her Cheerios, she appeared to be thinking about something. After a bit, Honey went to the water dish and pushed it with her beak a little toward Lily. She stopped—waited—and again pushed it even closer to Lily. With another hefty push, Honey positioned the water dish exactly where Lily was eating the Cheerios. With her eyes gleaming, Honey nudged the water dish with just enough strength so that it was aimed directly at Lily. After one last push of the dish, Honey gripped the rim with her beak and lifted it up so that water splashed all over the dry Cheerios—and Lily! Quickly, Lily's taste buds for Cheerios turned back to seeds.

Oh dear, this is not a good way to start this beautiful day, I thought to myself. Anyway, Honey and Lily convinced me to get my own bowl of Cheerios. I considered myself lucky that I didn't have to share Cheerios with Honey.

Also, another gastronomical delight of the avian cuisine is popcorn, as it is of mine. One afternoon I decided to have a light snack. I searched my cupboard and espied a box of popcorn I had bought the previous month but had forgotten it was still stored in the cupboard. So, I took a single packet out and stuck it in the microwave oven for a couple of minutes to pop. As the corn pop—pop—popped, I heard much chirping and movement in the bird cage. I checked on the birds to see what all the excitement was about. They paced back and forth on the perches. As I talked to the birds, the microwave oven beeped to let me know the popcorn was done. So, I went back to the kitchen and I thought to myself, *Ooooh, who can't love the tantalizing smell of fresh popped corn?* Well, I quickly learned I was not alone in enjoying this treat. I dished up the popcorn and decided to offer some to Honey and Lily. They immediately jumped down from their perches, with their wings fluttering rapidly in excitement. As I opened the doors to each food dish area, they nudged and nipped at each other with their beaks, vying to eat from the palm of my hand before I could even put the popcorn in the first of their dishes. I already thought that they would like uncooked popcorn, but apparently their appetite for the white, puffed corn was almost as great as mine as they eagerly ate this treat.

The birds now seemed to know when I was about to have a popcorn snack. As soon as they heard the sounds of the cellophane packet being opened, they began chirping and pacing on their perches. They apparently understood that when the clock timer dinged from the microwave oven, the corn was ready. Then the adrenalizing aroma was the real tip-off. They knew their favorite snack would come soon. Every time we prepared popcorn, they became excited with their chattering and rapid movements inside the cage. Needless to say, the popcorn did not stay in the cupboard for any considerable length of time as it had done in the past. As I watched the birds eat the popcorn, I knew our love for this special treat was mutual.

Cousins

One evening, as I was working at my computer, I received an e-mail message from Achilles. He was also working at his computer, but in another room of the house. The e-mail contained a video attachment of a breeding location's film of cockatiels.

As I began to view the video, Achilles joined me at my computer workstation, and we watched the filmed cockatiels begin their efforts to mate. After they jumped over each other several times, they finally got into the right position. Suddenly, outside the camera's view, two other cockatiels flew on the scene, which startled the birds in the romantic connection and abruptly halted the planned mating.

While we viewed this video in one room, Honey and Lily listened in a nearby room.

In the video, the two uninvited cockatiels began to scream and screech. When Honey and Lily heard their cousins' voices, they began responding to the filmed cockatiels' voices. Each time the filmed birds spoke, Honey and Lily recognized cousins' voices, and they began returning friendly calls to them. The conversation between the filmed and live cockatiels was so funny that Achilles and I just couldn't stop laughing at this interaction.

Later in the evening, when Angelo finished in his workshop, Achilles and I replayed the film for him to view and enjoy. Again, when the filmed cockatiels began their bird chatter, Honey and Lily would reply. We decided that Honey and Lily seemed to know that these were distant cousins that they were hearing, that they must have returned, and they were happy again to converse with them.

Our precious and fascinating cockatiels often bring many spontaneous and humorous moments to our household.

Honey and Lily Perched Atop the Chariot of the
Mythological Athenian God, Achilles

Epilogue

As of December, 2011, more than four years have passed since the miraculous find of Honey—though barely alive—and the joyous arrival of Lily.

We have celebrated another Christmas season. Again, the house was decorated with Christmas ornaments and colorful lights. Both birds showed wonderment as they saw themselves reflected in the decorations, and they were dazzled by the bright flashing lights. Neither bird flew to the Christmas tree to perch on the top as our tree-topper, Honey, had done in the past. We smiled and enjoyed the new Christmas music that Honey and Lily made by adding their lilting, cheerful sounds to the musical scores.

We continued to watch Honey for healthy signs of recovery in memory. Physically, she slowly revived into the beautiful cockatiel we remembered. Life gleams back into her eyes. She welcomes us to gently hold her and lightly kiss her. She returns our kisses with soft pecks, an indication we are gaining her trust.

Honey's body remains small in size. She is not as strong in flight; she tires easily. Many of her delightful traits have not returned; for example, she no longer sits on Achilles' shoulder or head. She does not seem to remember flying down the hall to Achilles' room nor combing his hair with her beak. This is sad for my son because he misses those happy carefree times. However, he is grateful that Honey is safe at home and remembers as much as she does.

Honey's call out to beckon Achilles no longer is as forceful and distinct. Lily learned from her how to beckon him for attention. Now, it is often impossible to distinguish which bird is doing the beckoning. Sometimes it sounds like they are competing to see which one will be the first to get his attention.

Honey enjoys coming out of the cage and flying around with Lily. They fly back and forth from their cage in the living room to the tops of the cupboards in the kitchen. Some of their flight maneuvers actually seem synchronized, almost as if they're performing their own personal air show.

Also amusing is their display of kissing. Honey is usually the first to move up close to Lily to seek a kiss. It seems like she is asking for permission. When Lily is in the mood, they begin kissing nonstop for periods up to a minute at a time. Sometimes their kissing is for shorter periods. Other times I think, *When will they come up for air?* Their kissing noises sound like our squeaky, washing-machine cycles. When they abruptly stop this act of affection, they each turn their faces around and look at us with guilt-like expressions. They seem to be embarrassed—either due to their lack of privacy or because they were caught in the act of doing something naughty. Afterwards, they go back to chatting in light, cheerful tones. These acts of affection reassure us of their happy and contented companionship.

Although Honey's body and memory will probably never fully recover, she is steadily improving from her traumatic experience. "Mama Lily" is ten years younger but remains Honey's staunch and faithful nursemaid, her doting and caring companion, and her perfect soul mate.

Afterword

R-r-r-ring! R-r-r-ring! As busy as Sunday mornings are, I was unable to answer the phone immediately and let the answering machine do its duty. Reminiscent of a past early Sunday morning phone call, I listened warily to the recorded phone message. The unusual call on this day was from our dentist's office secretary, Joanne. She was aware that I was in the process of writing this book, *Feather Faith*, relating to experiences with our cockatiels. Joanne's message informed me that her neighbor's dearly beloved cockatiel had escaped through the neighbor's opened patio doors two or three days earlier. The neighbor lived on a five-acre piece of property. The cockatiel was still on her property but staying perched very high in the densely wooded tree tops. The owner had not had the cockatiel's wings clipped, as suggested in books on the care of cockatiels. Joanne wondered if I had useful suggestions to lure the liberated bird down.

Not being a professional bird handler, I suggested that they contact one, possibly at an animal control shelter. As I thought this was unusual for the bird to still be on the owner's property, I suggested that the owner might attach some special bird treats to the bird's opened cage and place it outdoors where her bird could see it. The owner did this for several days. Other birds welcomed this opportunity to feed on these special treats. On the sixth day the cockatiel had been loose, the owner again placed the opened bird cage outdoors with its treat attached thereon. On this day, the owner sat outside near the cage and called the cockatiel's name repeatedly. Finally, the bird flew down and alighted in the bush next to where the owner sat. The frantic owner breathed a huge sigh of relief as she reached to recover her beloved pet.

In less than three weeks of the above incident, another unexpected event occurred on our property. My husband was busy placing new tomato plants in our freshly plowed spring garden. As he reached down to pack the soil around the plants, suddenly he heard soft sounds going, "Peep, peep, peep." As he searched the area for this soft sound—lo and behold—about three feet from where he was standing, he was amazed to see a new bird he had not seen in our yard before. (Angelo strews wild bird seed out daily for the wild birds in our yard so he is very familiar with myriad bird sounds.) Angelo called to me to come to the garden. When I arrived in the back yard, Angelo beckoned me to see the new bird, which he had temporarily covered with a food strainer. *We must have an invisible sign on our property that reads—The Papadatos Bird Sanctuary,* I thought to myself as I approached the bird. I soon realized the latest bird in the garden's spotlight turned out to be a very small blue parakeet—another owner's poor, lost pet! We did not know how long it had been outdoors, and it did not appear to be afraid. I got an empty shoe box and placed the bird inside. Our cockatiels began chattering excitedly when they heard the parakeet peeping as I entered the house. I did not put the parakeet in the cage with our cockatiels because our birds were somewhat larger in size, as well as I wanted to be careful that, if this bird had an unknown bird disease, it would not be transferred between the two species. I fed it some of our cockatiels' bird seeds and gave it water to drink. It appeared to be very hungry. By now, I knew what I had to do next—call the local animal control shelter to report this found beauty. Now I felt it was our turn to be the Good Samaritan as another family had been for us. When my son arrived home from work that evening, he delivered the parakeet to the animal shelter, where they hold lost pets for thirty days for owners to claim their lost pets. If pets are not claimed within that timeframe, they are allowed to be adopted by others.

Unfortunately, these incidents are more common than one would realize. They require responsible care-givers to be educated and prepared to react immediately when unexpected accidents happen, such as these, and as experienced in *Feather Faith*.

Birds, as all pets, are especially endearing to us. As stressful as these accidents are for pet owners, they are also stressful for their pets. After several days out of a cockatiel's safe cage, tamed birds, as in this case, become confused. Their bodies begin to shrink in size because they are not receiving the normal amounts of nutrition and water to which they have been acclimated—not to mention the role their emotions play in these stressful events. Therefore, while we owners love our pets dearly, we must adhere to professional guidance and advice as to their proper care. Clipping cockatiels' wings prevent accidents. For example, wings that have been clipped still allow birds the ability to fly, but they are constrained from flying great distances. This enables owners an optimistic chance of capturing their pets. If owners are uncomfortable administering and maintaining this care for birds, they should seek the aid from professionals. Because we reap so much love and joy from these beautiful creatures, we must remember to ensure their safety by performing these necessary responsibilities.

About the Author

In 1973, **Bonnie S. Papadatos** met her husband to be, Evangelos, on her one and only Greek cruise. They married in 1974, and their only son, Achilles, was born on July 4, 1983. She retired after completing extensive administrative careers with the Government and a religious entity, respectively. She is an avid reader and has always adored pets. Originally from Michigan, she now resides in Virginia with her husband, son, and their beloved pet cockatiels.